Heart F

Songs of the Heart

Ana Lisa de Jong

Living Tree Poetry

BOOK PUBLISHING

langbookpublishing.com

National Library of New Zealand Cataloguing-in-Publication Data.

Lang Book Publishing 2018.

ISBN 978-1-98-855710-6 – Softback
ISBN 978-1-98-855709-0 – Hardback
ISBN 978-1-98-855711-3 – eBook

Published in New Zealand.

A catalogue record for this book is available from the National Library of New Zealand.

Kei te pātengi raraunga o Te Puna Mātauranga o Aotearoa te whakarārangi o tēnei pukapuka.

To friends near and far.
Words are a way to heaven.
Thank you for joining me on the journey.

Capturing beauty with the camera is another way to heaven,
and I thank my dear friend Carol Haines
whose stunning photography accompanies mine in this book.

I thanked God for you
and He said,

'They are simply Me,
come to you through a thousand
different means,
and counting.

I love you through your friends,
and that person on the street
that smiled,
and the brush of next door's cat
against your skin.

Counting?
You cannot measure all the
ways I love you.
But begin.

And keep measuring.
As the sun will rise tomorrow
I come again, and again,
and again.'

Ana Lisa de Jong

CONTENTS

PART 2: SING

PART 3: SHOUT

INTRODUCTION

Poetry is an expression of the heart's journey. For the spiritual writer, writing regularly means there is a record kept, an account made, a collation created of the 'songs' of the heart, the 'breathings' of the spirit, and the 'yearnings' of the soul over a period of time. An account which testifies to the joys and struggles, faith and doubt-filled moments of daily life, and an awareness of God's presence, made even more tangible and real, by the record that has been kept of it.

Within that record, for the spiritual writer, there are also the 'songs' of God's heart that he sings over us. Threads of gold weaved through the pattern of the days, laid out in words, meanings to be discerned and understood as we attempt to unwrap what has been given.

Beyond that, there is also the awareness that sometimes we hold the privilege of tapping into a common song, whether of lament or hope, or joyful praise. And still again, on those occasions that we compose the words right, God may even seek to use our pen, as an instrument to communicate to the hearts of his creation, with a message from his own.

For myself, the 'Heart Psalms' in this collection have also been inspired by the 'Book of Psalms', one of the most read and re-read books of the Bible, for those of us who seek a record of his faithfulness, through challenge and adversity, who need honest words that go some way towards conveying our own struggles, and brokenness. And for those times we seek a song of praise to echo our own heart's response to God in worship, the Psalms provide that for many of us too.

It is my prayer that this book, in some way, might act as a resource, an instrument to recalibrate our hearts towards one another and God and to absorb his message of constancy, and changelessness, in a world of turmoil, change and inconstancy. The three sections of the book follow the themes that weave through our lives in varying patterns, from grief, loneliness and struggle, to optimism, anticipation and hope, to joy, confidence and celebration.

This book of songs is a complete song in itself. With depth and height, and notes short and long. Each note makes sense of the other notes. All are needed to make a rich, deep resounding music.

Sing with me.

Ana Lisa de Jong
Living Tree Poetry
January 2018

"We're an ongoing part of the revelation of God's heart. We're where God's heart is happening."

Cynthia Bourgeault

PART 1: STILL

'I will go to the altar of God, to God, my joy and my delight.
I will praise you with the lyre, O God, my God.
Why, my soul, are you downcast?
Why so disturbed within me?
Put your hope in God, for I will yet praise him,
my Saviour and my God.'

Psalm 43:4-5 (NIV)

HEART SONG

I had hung up my harp
but my God still demands a song.
'How can I draw a note?' I asked,
my heart within grown cold.

I have weighed justice and mercy
until mercy has hardly registered,
and bitterness become a weight
that kept me counting my losses.

But we are asked to hold all things lightly.
Despair and hope can both draw notes
in hands that recognise the qualities
of height and depth, light and dark needed to make music.

Have you hung up your harp?
Will you take it up again with me?
Together we can extract the gold
we can yet mine from sorrow.

And hope can rise from the ashes of today
to make a brand new song.
Together we can draw meaning from all
that befalls us, good or ill.

We have stilled our hearts
but God can thaw the fingers which refuse to bend.
Until they move again
as dancers on the strings.

Of our harps, which because of hope we have taken down.
Because hope, unlike anything else we encounter,
springs eternal in our souls
that we might each, always have a song.

'By the rivers of Babylon we sat and wept when we remembered Zion.
There on the poplars we hung our harps,
for there our captors asked us for songs,
our tormentors demanded songs of joy; they said,
"Sing us one of the songs of Zion!"
How can we sing the songs of the Lord while in a foreign land?
If I forget you, Jerusalem, may my right hand forget its skill. May my
tongue cling to the roof of my mouth if I do not remember you, if I do not
consider Jerusalem my highest joy.'

Psalm 137:1-6 (NIV)

DARK

What do you want me to do with this morning God?
That shines through the blinds.
That shines through my shuttered heart.

What do I do with a sun that still rises?
On us, whose joy wavers as a candle in the wind.
On those, whose joy has for a moment, been snuffed out.

What do we do with fear that lurks at the edges?
As dark clouds that threaten to bring more rain,
as though we hadn't yet had enough of the dark.

Yet the sun rises,

shedding all vestiges of where she has been,
illuminating the shadows to reveal them as naught but things
that take on power in the absence of the light.

Things that have always been
but that we too can brush off
at the arrival of the dawn.

For hope and love too have always been
and resilience, and prayer, and hearts
that constantly strive for good.

What do we do with this morning God?
That shines through the blinds
and breaks apart our shattered hearts.

We rise like the sun
and we shed our light into the dark.

'Neither do people light a lamp and put it under a bowl.
Instead they put it on its stand, and it gives light to everyone in the house.
In the same way, let your light shine...'

Matthew 5:15-17 (NIV)

TEARS

Tears that fall
become a river
which flows ever forward.

To flood
the fertile soil
at water's edge.

And soak the thirsty
parched earth
with its rivulets.

Tears that fall
become a sea
upon which we surface.

To breathe
upon the wide
expansive waters.

To see
the new breadth
from a cleansed perspective.

To rest
upon the bark
that always carries us.

And to feel the sun,
new again,
upon cleansed skin.

Just as our world
showered upon
appears the cleaner, so we

with tears
are washed afresh
to see with extra clarity.

Yes, tears that fall
become a river
to forever buoy us up.

Never fear
the pain or grief
that draws them to emerge.

Let them
but seep
into the thirsty earth.

'You keep track of all my sorrows.
You have collected all my tears in your bottle.
You have recorded each one in your book.'

Psalm 56:8 (NIV)

WE GRIEVE

We grieve

but there is a love
stronger than death,
greater than the life
given in this mortal breath.

We grieve

but there is life
in a larger sense
that exceeds the limits of
our human experience.

There is peace
beyond the grave,
deeper than the quiet
of this temporal plane.

There is hope
higher than the sky,
lengths of thread
unfurled beyond our sight.

Though we grieve

there is faith
in mankind, despite ourselves.
In each other,
beyond the losses of today.

We are asked to love,
when love is hardest
and restore the life for each other,
that is taken away.

To be the peace and hope
that would be stolen,
as if peace were a fleeting gift
and hope up for the taking.

For our peace and love,
hope and life,
spring from a fountain
fed by an eternal source.

We grieve

but await the answers
to our questions.
We are not without a reason
or a purpose for our remaining.

We are not without
a morning,
to burn away the darkness of
today.

'My flesh and my heart may fail,
but God is the strength of my heart
and my portion forever.'

Psalm 26:76 (NIV)

BE STILL

Be still.
Be still and know
that I am God.

Be still for I am he
who's in you,
and I'm greater than all
in this world.

Be still for I am here
within you,
holding you up
so you cannot fall.

Be still because I will
deliver you.
Not one moment too late,
nor too soon.

And in the meantime,

when it's hard to do anything else.
When it feels too daunting
to take one step
left or right.

Then I will lead
from up front,
and I will support
you from behind.

You can do it,
those things you think you cannot do.
Just rest in me
as you walk.

Just be still.

'I wait for the Lord, my whole being waits,
and in his word I put my hope.'

Psalm 130:5 (NIV)

A HARBOUR

We need a harbour.

A harbour where we can moor our vessels
that have been tossed and turned
by inclement weather,
by changing currents
and the wear and tear
of all our endeavours.

We need a place where we can shed ourselves.
Selves, which like the colour on our lips,
have worn thin with too much time
between our attentions.
Have started to need more effort to sustain
than we can spare.

Then we need a place
where we can go to restore and mend.
We need the shoulders of the Comforter.
The body of his house.
The refuge of his courts, where he meets us, inestimable host,
as though we had never been gone.

We need a harbour.
Where we can take our longings, our endless needs,
to the edge and pour them in.
That wraps its presence around us
and reminds us, indeed we need nothing
that isn't already ours, here, in this place.

This place in which he is
the centre piece.

'How lovely is your dwelling place, Lord Almighty! My soul yearns, even
faints, for the courts of the Lord: my heart and my flesh cry out for the
living God. Even the sparrow has found a home, and the swallow a nest
for herself, where she may have her young—a place near your altar, Lord
Almighty, my King and my God. Blessed are those who dwell in your
house; they are ever praising you. Blessed are those whose strength is in
you, whose hearts are set on pilgrimage. As they pass through the Valley of
Baka, they make it a place of springs; the autumn rains also cover it with
pools. They go from strength to strength,
till each appears before God in Zion.'

Psalm 84 (NIV)

ABIDE

Abide

with me.
Be still and know that
I am.

Have charted

your path.
Made room and
time for refreshment.

No, don't resist.

There is no struggle
in the bird
that nestles close.

I am

a jealous God.
Yet you strive
and rush.

Forgetting

we were meant,
at our core,
for relationship.

So abide with me.

Be still and know,
I am yet,
and always shall be,

the God
who calls you to himself.

'By this we know that we abide in him, and he in us,
because he has given us of his Spirit.'

1 John 4:13 (NIV)

SAD

There is something immensely sad
resounding in the depths
and carrying on the airwaves,
that is finding a response in us.
The groaning of the earth
is felt by the sensitive.

We don't know what we are listening for
but we hear it.
We don't know what is moving us
but we register it.
Other's tears we brush from our own cheeks.
Other's wounds run fresh with our blood.

We are intrinsically connected.

While the waves jolt us
and the earth appears even to expel us,
as if we were superfluous,
we are still rocked in unison.
The tide carries us in one direction.
We make landfall on a common shoreline.

One person's healing becomes another's hope.
One person's hope is sowed as a seed
to grow in the heart of the other,
until love takes root, and
sprouts as the tree that heals the nations
and the broken earth.

Yes, there is something immensely sad
resounding in the depths
and carrying on the airwaves.
There is an ache, a worry at the edges of our thoughts,
that we might recognise what it is we fear
and yet name the shapes we see in the dark.

But for light, we might indeed be lost.
But hand in hand we carry a torch each
that from our hands will never be knocked.
Not while your tears are brushed
from my wet cheeks,
and my heart healed by your love.

'On each side of the river stood the tree of life,
bearing twelve crops of fruit, yielding its fruit every month.
And the leaves of the tree are for the healing of the nations.'

Revelation 22:2 (NIV)

WORDLESS

Loss is so deep,
there are no words
to define its meaning
that we can speak.

It is empty,

like the ringing of a bell gone silent,
or the rush of the bird
that all of a sudden
takes flight.

We are left alone,
and that alone is overwhelming.

We can no longer stand up.
We cannot speak.

But love has not flown.

Though we stand without
the substance of a person in our life,
or thing, whatever it is,
that like the tide
has departed at our feet,

love still exists.

It is the only given.

And it restores the floor
under us
where we lost our footing.
It's in the hands that uplift us
in our grief.

The love that we have lost
can't be replaced.
There's still that hole.
We cannot circumnavigate our grief.

But love transforms.

The tree that flourished
and then lost its leaves
has dropped its crown.
But its seeds

lie buried in the ground
beneath.

Our loss can still co-exist
with life.
We see spring emerge from winter
and dawn from
the darkest night.

Our hearts may break,
but the breaking brings
its own healing.
Grief will not consume us complete.

In that day that light brings
its blessed relief,
we will find its love
that kept us from

falling.

'So we do not lose heart. Though our outer self is wasting away,
our inner self is being renewed day by day.
For this light momentary affliction
is preparing for us an eternal weight of glory beyond all comparison,
as we look not to the things that are seen but to the things that are unseen.
For the things that are seen are transient, but the things that are unseen
are eternal.'

2 Corinthians 4:16-18 (NIV)

LENT

'Giving God,
what do I give up
this Lent?

For you

who reminds me that
everything you have
given us is lent.

Fashioned

only for what
it was meant.
A reason, a season or a day.

Everything is yours to give
and take away.

Giving God,
what do I release to you
this Lent?

My questions,

my answers, and
the prayers uttered
until I am spent.

Wondering

why do you not
give us what we want?
Instead, you will

that we should give
to you our all.

That empty,
we might count our benefits.'

'Humble yourselves, therefore, under God's mighty hand,
that he may lift you up in due time.'

1 Peter 5:6 (NIV)

AH

Ah, I thought,
I love everything.
The summer sun,
the leaves on the shimmering trees,
the breeze
through the open window.

But the fleeting fantail
that just flew to alight
on the branch
teaches me, that life
and its gifts
run ever out.

A closed fist
holds nothing of worth,
while an open hand,
though its treasures run out
through its fingers,
contains everything.

'One gives freely, yet grows all the richer;
another withholds what he should give,
and only suffers want.'

Proverbs 11:24 (NIV)

PEACE STARTS HERE

Peace must start here,
in the battlefield of our hearts,
where our wills seek their way
and our wants collide with others.

Peace must be brokered
in the dark of our thoughts,
where our wounds lie exposed
to our bitter judgements.

Yes, peace must be sought
in the ashes of our anger,
where we sift through the wreckage
for what can be salvaged.

But as long as we seek
reasons for our anger to be justified,
or even look for evidence
that we can put it aside,

while we seek things redeeming
in our neighbour's eyes,
we miss the point of peace,
and we will never find it.

For peace is only brokered
when we give up our positions.
When we recognise that each of us
will never be right.

Though our neighbour
may hurt us, and justice be denied,
our standpoint's also wrong,
when cemented by our pride.

For peace is gentle,
and its power is in the unexpected
way that it dilutes the enemy's ability
to wound us.

Christ poured his blood
out for those who did not deserve it.
And we stand on the ground
of those who died before us.

Who cry out not for vengeance
but for us to restore
that for which they once fought,
and fell.

And it starts
not on the streets, or the battle-lines
so dearly bought,
but in the resolve of our minds

and our hearts.

> 'They must turn from evil and do good;
> they must seek peace and pursue it.'
>
> 1 Peter 3:11 (NIV)

WINNERS AND LOSERS

When you wound me
I wound you.

When I wound you
I wound me.

When you wound me
you wound you.

There is no one of us who wins,
there are only two who lose.

Because we meet in the middle by a sea
that laps at both of our shores.

When you love me
I love you.

When I love you
I love me.

When you love me
you love you.

There is no one of us who wins,
there are two of us who do.

Because we meet in the middle by a sea
that connects my heart to yours.

Will you love with me?
Leave the blame behind?

We have a boat to carry us both,
wounded though we might be.

'Let us therefore make every effort to do
what leads to peace and to mutual edification.'

Romans 14:19 (NIV)

I WEAVE

I weave.

I never stop stitching
what you unstitch.
I never stop repairing
what you tear.

I mend.

Frayed edges
and holes on knees.
Those places you're rubbed raw,
I take and restore.

Gently, tenderly,

I come behind,
carrying the thread.
I put together what had you undone.
I tend to each of your needs.

I weave.

I weave together,
all the loose ends.
You won't unravel
in me.

I mend.

'Jerusalem is built like a city that is closely
compacted together.'

Psalm 122:3 (NIV)

ASCENSION

'Keep going, don't give up', I read.

Yet keeping going today
looks something like,
closing and opening my eyes,
and turning over to my other side
in bed.

Progress is sometimes measured
in the smallest increments.

My not giving up today
was perhaps seen
in the leap of my heart,
at the tui and fantail on the branches
beyond my window's ledge.

Sometimes progress is measured by the reach of our vision,
beyond the place we now rest.

'Stop, go.'
Who is asking that we maintain our pace?
To rest is to regain the strength to rise.
Before we release a breath,
we must breathe in the oxygen we need.

Yes, our hearts,
they beat to the measure of our supplies.

So sometimes not giving up
looks like curling into a cocoon,
and drawing the blankets in tight.
We might need to tend
and mend ourselves,

as the cat that comes in from the night
licks at its wounds.

The shelter of the cocoon
provides the supports that aid our healing.
Before we ascend,
we must kneel and bend
to get the uplift desired.

No, we don't give up,
and keep, however slowly, making ground.

But it's not clear cut.

Sometimes ascending looks a lot
like slowing down.

'…Jesus often withdrew to lonely
places and prayed.'

Luke 5:6 (NIV)

EXCEPT A GRAIN OF WHEAT

Except a grain of wheat

fall, catch the current of the wind,
and lose all sense of direction,
to rest in a place unbidden and foreign,
it remains a single grain.

Yet, unbridled or contained,
and at the mercy of God's faithfulness,
it bears the seed for the new season's harvest.
It becomes new bread.

Yes, I think it is that what often looks like death,
or lack of fruitfulness, is instead,
just the time it takes
for the gift of life to flourish.

And tears, and gestures, or words,
the frustrated expressions
from good intents gone vaguely wrong,
or not as we would have determined,

the love that appears to be in vain;
they bear our heart's cries as seed.
While God's purposes he sometimes shields,
from our current understanding.

So that just like grain, or leaves,
or anything that falls,
we find next season's yield,
is often stored,

in the remains of the first.
Apparent death just the shedding
of the husk,
that brings about new birth.

'Very truly I tell you, unless a kernel of wheat falls to the ground and dies,
it remains only a single seed. But if it dies, it produces many seeds.'

John 12:24 (NIV)

FALLING

I am falling
like the rain.
Like the light through the broken clouds.

I am falling
like a leaf
whose time it is to drop.

Like a musical note
carried aloft
to your ear and mine.

I am falling like the sun.

Like someone
who realises there are no more supports
for the weight we carry,

which we voluntarily adopt.

I am falling
into grace
and love that has no boundaries,

but draws me from my feet
to the floor, where I bow in reverence
to the one who holds me up.

I am falling,
but to the relief
that comes from knowing

I am carried on the currents of the wind,
to greater and greater
freedom.

The return of those who give up
their rights
and fall that they might gain.

For those who hit the floor
to find a universe
under their feet.

*'For you have been my help, and in the shadow of your wings
I will sing for joy. My soul clings to you;
your right hand upholds me.'*

Psalm 63:7-8 (NIV)

A FIELD

Rumi said, 'there is a field',
out beyond yonder somewhere.
There is a place beyond right and wrong.
I tell myself, when I'm held down
by lead feet to the unforgiving ground,

that there's a field.

That I can roll off the weights
and find myself unshackled.
That in the end the only reason I stay bound
is that I tie myself too tight in knots.
I must come unwound.

Then this field,

that I search so very hard to reach,
I might just find, finds me.
That I might rise to meet it someplace,
turn around and find myself in thin air.
As maybe it's not far from here at all.

Meet you there?

'Blessed are those who believe without seeing.'

John 20:29 (NIV)

PERFECT

Don't wait for the perfect.
Life is here right now.

Shadows and light,
the losses and the gains,
make a rich fabric of our days.

Depth discerned by a light in the dark,
that we hold like a lantern
and pick our way.

The shadows across the river's face
give a hue I would never see
if all were bright.

Greens that mirror a changing sky.
Rich shades reflecting
filtered light.

And the Monarch Butterfly
that flicks its wings
so fleetingly across my vision;

its colour stands out
in greater clarity,
for the darkness of its edge.

Don't wait for the perfect.
We're all too afraid we'll miss it
if we close our eyes and blink.

Oh but we won't,
for it comes disguised in the greys,
to which we need just be present.

'And I will give you treasures hidden in the darkness
--secret riches.'

Isaiah 45:3 (NIV)

A BEGGAR

I am a beggar at your door,
the steps rising before my hesitant feet.

I can hear the sounds within
your kingdom drawing me,

despite my lack of confidence.
My feet unclean,

I could wipe them more than once
and they would still not shed

the grime.

So I turn and sit at the foot
of your steps,

content if I hear nothing
else but the sounds of this place.

If I do not move from here.
For this is where I feel at ease,

one foot in and one foot out,
not to soil the floor of a house

too good for me.

I am beggar, come hopeful guest,
and you know I am here.

More aware of those without
than within,

those who waver at the door,
not trusting their right to enter.

And you come to find me,
leaving your guests to usher in

those that linger at the entrance.

The dirt of my feet
you don't tend to mind,

although you patiently wait
as I scrape at the earth.

And my clothes, seen too much wear for me,
you cover with a robe of lamb's wool,

whiter than the last of the snow
blanketing the hills.

And then you take my hand and grasp tight in welcome.

As though I had not been gone,
as though there were no question of my belonging

here, in this kingdom,
wider within than without.

With walls extending
beyond the extent of my vision.

Roof higher than my eyesight's reach
and a table longer than comprehension,

where guests sit joyous and replete.

That I might be one of them?
That I might find my place set?

Is always the silent question,
at the fore-front of my mind.

But without doubt
you know the answer.

You, who have come to seek those
who think themselves lost.

You hold a spot vacant

bearing my name.

'Blessed is the one who will eat at
the feast in God's kingdom.'

Luke 14:15 (NIV)

THE DOOR

Faith is a key.
Fear is a lock.

Faith, the fabric that covers me.
Fear, the incessant cold.

Faith, the shield
fear's arrows clear

and the one
who seeks for me.

Until faith then
becomes the door

I go in and out
restored.

'Be strong and courageous.
Do not be afraid; do not be discouraged,
for the Lord your God will be with you wherever you go.'

Joshua 1:9 (NIV)

THE ROAD

I was afraid
that the road was too narrow.
That myself and my load
could not together pass.

Then I was afraid
it might in fact be too wide.
That I would turn in circles
and miss the landmarks.

I was afraid
it might at times give out.
That what I believed was a road
was instead a track to naught.

I was afraid to walk.
Afraid to point others
to this road or that,
as right.

Had I not thought that roads
were a path to follow.
That they needed strict observance
to a map.

But then in relief
I felt my heart held,
in hands that were
both loose and tight.

My gracious guide
revealed the road was not
a maze that we must in earnest
navigate.

It is a way of life.
A relaxing into arms that bear us up.
Where-ever the road takes me,
He is at my feet and side.

'For I will bring them from the north and from earth's farthest ends, not
forgetting their blind and lame, young mothers with their little ones, those
ready to give birth. It will be a great company who comes. Tears of joy
shall stream down their faces, and I will lead them home with great care.
They shall walk beside the quiet streams and not stumble.
For I am a Father to Israel.'

Jeremiah 31:8-9 (NIV)

TURN POINTS

We don't always know which road to take,

although we perceive your face at every bend.
The way unclear slowly reveals
to our eyes, so slow to discern,

that which-ever option we choose to take,
even that of staying put,
you always wait for us, with utmost courtesy.

As though we didn't have time to make up.
As though the world weren't awaiting us to act
(as though to act were always the answer).

And as we stand at the pivot point
of left, and right, advance and retreat,
we come to understand our goals might be different to yours.

Maybe the outcome and our destinations
are not nearly so important as the truth that you wait just ahead,
that you might walk with us where-ever we turn.

'The Lord is my shepherd, I shall not lack.'

Psalm 23:1 (NIV)

SUN ON SNOW

I wish for you,

sunshine on snow.
A pass where there is
no passageway.
A means to proceed.

And I pray,

for frozen rivers that thaw,
that burst their banks
with showers of mercy
and blessing.

Sometimes I wonder
if he is more purposeful
than we quite
understand.

That he makes our way hard,
or dark, or confusing,
that he might come through
with a plan.

Like sunshine on snow,
or passes that clear,
and rivers of blessing
to break barriers.

So God's mercy,
when it bursts its banks,
carries us
in its forward momentum.

'When I said, "My foot is slipping," your unfailing love,
Lord, supported me.
When anxiety was great within me, your consolation brought me joy.'

Psalm 94:18-19 (NIV)

FLIGHT

God taught me of love.
How it was a like a kite
that you lengthen and let loose.
Or the string of a bow
that sets an arrow on its path.

In no way did he teach me
it was something to be kept.
Rather it was something that you
kept on giving out,
like the loosening strings of a kite.

You don't know where the
wind will take your love.
It might whip far and wide
and then return to you in an arc.
Whatever, your love is going where it's meant.

Its place isn't to stay
bound in your heart,
or in a neat little box all tied up.
Love finds its full expression
in the giving up.

In the lengthening out.
We were made not to keep
one another in our sight.
For the reach of love's as far
as daytime is from night.

We love most when we realise
the gift in giving up.
How it's not the tight rein
that maintains our control.
But the loose hand

that holds each other up
in flight.

'Now the Lord is the Spirit, and where the Spirit
of the Lord is, there is freedom.'

2 Corinthians 3:17 (NIV)

LOVE'S DEMANDS

Love is in the breaking
and the putting back together.
It is in the heart that hurts
and the ribs that protect,

and tether us together.

It is not as soft as we might believe.
Though it's the most gentle thing
in earth and heaven.
It is in the roots that anchor a tree,

and the leaves that move to the wind.

And we must move with love
to know that it expands,
even while its feet
stay attached to the ground.

Our hearts

have their ebb and flow.
Pain and joy, frustration, gratitude;
we live exposed and at the mercy
of love's demands.

Yes, if we are to understand at all,

we must see it as the seed that bursts.
For it is in the little deaths
that we make it something else
stronger still.

It evolves.

And we like the tree,
that in the summer blossom and fruit,
nurture and shelter,
in the winter sometimes must

stand alone.

Learning in leanness,
that life is fruitfulness;
the giving and the yielding,
the waiting and the receiving.

We can't keep anything

but must move with love,
which in its creative force
won't leave us where
we might wish to remain.

It grows us to our heights.

It makes us drop our seeds
upon the ground.
It asks that we shed the shells
of ourselves,

to become the bread
that multiplies.

'"They do not need to go away. You give them something to eat." "We have here only five loaves of bread and two fish," they answered. "Bring them here to me," he said. And he directed the people to sit down on the grass. Taking the five loaves and the two fish and looking up to heaven, he gave thanks and broke the loaves. Then he gave them to the disciples, and the disciples gave them to the people. They all ate and were satisfied…'

Matthew 14:16-20 (NIV)

WE NEVER KNOW

We never know,

so there is never any choice
but to be kind.

We do not know,
so there is never any reason to assume we do,

or that we're right,
for we're often wrong,

and far from expert,
in our deductions.

We may never know,

so we must uphold others in their right to hold their own
counsel.

We cannot see into another's heart,
or give them words we would want them to say.

They are, and we are,
and only sometimes do we meet in that place between.

And that has to be enough.

At other times,

when we are strange ships that pass
too close for comfort, or oblivious at night,

then we are to trust
that what makes them human,

responds to the humanity
in us.

We are alike.
Alone in our uniqueness but none the less still in tune.

No, we never know.

But we are gracious as we remember how it is
that love

covers all our differences,
and gives us the freedom to exist

individually, and separate,
but linked.

Yes love it is
that gives us the power to be kind.

And kindness it is
that keeps such love alive.

'*Above all, love each other deeply,*
because love covers over a multitude of sins.'

1 Peter:4-8 (NIV)

GROWING PAINS

It hurts.

It hurts when the shell breaks
to make room for the new.

When the husk cracks
so that the green can push through.

It hurts when we're growing
beyond what our constraints can restrain.

Growth cannot be delayed
but pushes through, despite the pain.

I would like to tell you that this will end,
but life has a way of emerging from within.

Losses and mistakes,
you count them as though you were to blame.

Don't.
They're the breaking of you, in preparation

for all you'll become.

---

*'The Lord was with Samuel as he grew up,
and he let none of Samuel's words fall to the ground.'*

1 Samuel 3:19-20 (NIV)

TO WAIT

Waiting is active.

It takes breath,
both in and out,
and then the holding of it.

It takes a certain awareness
of the heart's race,
and the stilling of it.

It takes letting go
of regret,
or even anticipation.

Reviewing expectation
in light of
the empty present.

Which always holds more
than we can
see in it.

Waiting takes a certain type of vision,
that magnifies a moment
to draw out its essence.

In the end
we find that the wait requires gratitude
for what isn't yet.

And what is,
even when we're wanting more
than that.

Waiting means holding a moment
with reverence,
careful with its contents.

As water in the hands of the thirsty
we do not spill a drop,
until we exchange it for the next.

Yes, waiting is patience's
perfect work in us.
Gratitude brings its payment.

We might yet take a breath and see,
if what we need
isn't already apparent.

'For the revelation awaits an appointed time;
it speaks of the end and will not prove false.
Though it linger, wait for it;
it will certainly come and will not delay.'

Habakkuk 2:3 (NIV)

CLEAR

Blotted away
and swept clean.

Waters stilled
until they're clear.

I, and my sins,
beneath your hand.

For your sake,
not just mine.

Forgotten,
and forever unrecalled.

One who is forgiven little
loves not as much

as one
forgiven more.

It's our love for you
that is your desire

and which we
publically declare.

The promise of forgiveness
leads us to reveal

our naked selves,
and deep-seated shame.

To you, the one who hears us
for no reason but

there be no obstruction
between your heart and ours.

Not to chastise
do you incline your ear,

but to remind
us of our status,

our eternal
dwelling place.

Where muddied waters flow clear
in the current of your grace.

'I, even I, am he who blots out your transgressions, for my own sake,
and remembers your sins no more. Review the past for me,
let us argue the matter together; state the case for your innocence.'

Isaiah 43:25-26 (NIV)

EDEN

Oh Lord, you are too Holy.
How do we become clean?

Not by our own efforts
do you assure me,
but by immersing ourselves
into the holy stream.

Oh, holy stream,
wash over my stains.

So that when my God looks at me
he sees not the dirt of my hands,
not my sullied self
but one he has loved and made.

One he's loved and died for
that my life might be reclaimed.

That I might image him as polished silver,
or a river stone set in sand.
Maybe even a jewel,
alight as the morning star in his palm.

Or simply as one that walks with him
in the garden, again.

*'And they heard the sound of the Lord God
walking in the garden in the cool of the day,
and the man and his wife hid themselves
from the presence of the Lord God
among the trees of the garden.'*

Genesis 3:8 (NIV)

INSIDE OUT

We are broken,
but we are entirely intact.

We are shattered,
but still in one piece.

We are grieving,
but still wholly complete.

We are lost,
but found.

We leave the throng
and arrive in him.

We run,
but never for long.

We look left, or right,
within and without.

He is always there,
waiting for us to recognise

we are broken,
but held together by love.

Shattered,
but pieced together with tender intent.

Grieving,
but held from breaking apart.

Lost in ourselves,
but never to him.

Who finds the cracks and enters them,
to restore us from inside out.

'But we have this treasure in jars of clay to show that this all-surpassing power is from God and not from us. We are hard pressed on every side, but not crushed; perplexed, but not in despair; persecuted, but not abandoned; struck down, but not destroyed.

2 Corinthians 4:7-9 (NIV)

GOD OF SMALL THINGS

My God is the God of small things.

Seeds.
Newborn babies.

Nutshells that contain multiple truths
in humble small containers.

My God is the God of small beginnings.

Like breathing
or opening eyelids.

If we but move today
we can accomplish what he asks.

God, my God of swaddled babes
that fumble for the breast,

he teaches us the worth of
lying still in trust.

My God is the God of humble things.

Caves.
Beds of straw.

Lives that don't amount to much
if judged upon their origins.

My God, is the God of silent things.

Wombs.
Passages in the dark.

Quiet incubators, within which cells divide
and muscles stretch towards the light.

God, my God of birth pangs
and pain that finds release,

he teaches us that the dark
often precedes new life.

My God is the god of honed things.
Parred down.
Simplified.

A carpenter sanding back the wood
to reveal the grain beneath.

My God, is the God of beloved things.

Neglected.
Abandoned.

Rescued for nothing they have done
but because of a plan of redemption.

God, my God of Christmas coming
somehow the wonder of Advent

is knowing we need do nothing
but let new life be birthed in us.

'What shall we say the kingdom of God is like,
or what parable shall we use to describe it?
It is like a mustard seed, which is the smallest of all seeds on earth.
Yet when planted, it grows and becomes the largest of all garden plants,
with such big branches that the birds can perch in its shade.'

Mark 4:30-32 (NIV)

TUI – A POEM FOR WINTER SOLSTICE

Tui, with your white breast,
you dance on the flimsy limb,
and sing a song
that keeps me still and listening.

As the wind tosses the leaves
against a leaden winter sky,
I wonder you have a tune still
that causes your lone breast to rise.

I fear the cold that I can feel
in the blustery wind
has got into my bones,
never mind that I sit warm inside.

Yes today, I am aware
there are two ways of being.

And I wonder Tui, with your tune,
how you could have known,
that for a moment there
I'd forgotten

the notes that give us a song.

'Though the fig tree does not bud and there are no grapes on the vines,
though the olive crop fails and the fields produce no food,
though there are no sheep in the pen and no cattle in the stalls, yet I will
rejoice in the Lord...'
Habakkuk 3:17-18 (NIV)

PART 2: SING

'I will praise you with the harp for your faithfulness, my God;
I will sing praise to you with the lyre, Holy One of Israel.
My lips will shout for joy when I sing praise to you—
I whom you have delivered.
My tongue will tell of your righteous acts all day long...'

Psalm 71:22-24 (NIV)

WE SING

We sing.

We open our mouths
before dawn breaks,
because our hope
seeds in the dark.

And we believe
before we see,
the dawn that breaks through leaves
and gilds them gold.

We arise
in our hearts,
and so our voice
declares the light

before it arrives.

*'So what shall I do? I will pray with my spirit,
but I will also pray with my understanding; I will sing with my spirit,
but I will also sing with my understanding.'*

1 Corinthians 14:15 (NIV)

SONG

Songs have breath.

Music has width
and length,
and breadth.

Our voice has a sound still,
that can lift us beyond
our grief.

Our fingers still
can touch the notes
that bring release.

For God is not dead.

His love, wide and long,
and deep,
defies our measurement.

And when loss
lowers our utterances
to a mere wisp of breath,

he reclaims our voice,
that our fingers might strike the keys
that resonate yet with life.

For God is alive.

And music has breath.
All that we see perish
is transformed beyond our sight.

And the power of music
is in its means to communicate
what we can't understand yet.

So sing on my friend.
Sing on.

> 'Sing to the Lord a new song, his praise from the ends of the earth,
> you who go down to the sea, and all that is in it,
> you islands, and all who live in them.'

Isaiah 42:10 (NIV)

GRACE

What does it take to lift our spirit?

A bird's solitary flight
across an ocean blue.

Watching the quiet progress of the sun
across the canvas of the day,

or the moon's slow rise.

That does not deny the sun her place,
but which takes its turn,

that all might be graced.

That all might receive
nourishment,

in the way we are designed to draw
from a myriad of mercies,

that we all might be full.

'The Lord will guide you always;
he will satisfy your needs in a sun-scorched land
and will strengthen your frame. You will be like a well-watered garden,
like a spring whose waters never fail.'

Isaiah 58:11 (NIV)

HARD EDGES

God knew grace
to be our greatest need.

Before comfort.
Before success.

Grace that softens the hard edge.
The things that catch us in our step.

Grace that soothes the little stings.
The things that draw the threat of tears.

God knew grace
to be our urgent need.

The only thing to make our human state
a thing to bear with dignity.

So God gave grace.
Gives grace more than any other gift.

Gifts like love, forgiveness,
or the benefit of the doubt

have at their core
an element of grace.

Indeed, are all simply grace
by another name.

Such grace that
our needs get turned upon their head.

Upon his grace we reach and stand
as on scaffolding.

We survey a world clearer
in clarity.

We see everything sustained
by the one who tends our souls.

We respond to these graces
with an exhale of relief.

Life has its sharp corners
but they're softened at the edge.

Grace falls
as rain from heaven.

> '...he will come to us like the winter rains,
> like the spring rains that water the earth.'
>
> Hosea 6:3 (NIV)

HEAVEN

They tell me there is no heaven
on earth.
But I have found pieces
that resemble it,
and have put them together
with a bonding agent
made of hope and faith.

And love,
that when the sun strikes it
in a certain way,
the whole picture
comes alight,
as something
from another place.

They tell me there is a heaven
but it's not here.
While I am certain that I have
cast out my line
and drawn an ocean like the tide,
or the sky's blue expanse
around me like a wrap.

They tell me heaven
is far away.
But I think despite what we are warned
that sometimes we need look into the sun,
rather than away.
Then we might find what we are seeking
holds us in its gaze.

And as the sea reflects the blue sky
so that on a perfect day
we can't see a defined edge,
so heaven is imaged
in our humanness,
and our glory
mixed in
with the earth's.

'He sits enthroned above the circle of the earth,
and its people are like grasshoppers.
He stretches out the heavens like a canopy,
and spreads them out like a tent to live in.'

Isaiah 20:22 (NIV)

REVELATION

Unravelling
God lets down his hair,
that like a ladder to infinity
we might climb to grasp at things
yet too large for us.

Unfolding his scrolls
God lays his knowledge out upon the landscape
that, if we are quick, we may catch
a grain of truth
in the sun's slip behind the hill.

Might feel our heart filled
in the moment
the golden arch bridges the sky.
Feel we know and are known by
something 'other' than ourselves.

And although we turn
to filter what we have found
to find it run out,
lost behind some obstruction,
just as the sun lowers beyond our sight,

we are larger for the encounter.
And he, who keeps us searching
and climbing ladders to infinity,
is the silent lover
only desiring our response.

We who try to work out love
and measure knowledge
by what we have to gain
have got it sorely wrong.
We succumb to the one who never ceases to visit.

And trail after him over the hill.

'I don't pretend to know it all. I am quiet now before the Lord, just as a child is weaned from the breast. My begging has been stilled.'

Psalm 131:1-2 (NIV)

LIFE IS A CIRCLE

Life is a circle.
You can get on and off at any point.
You can fall and fail.
You can rest and deflate.
You can wait, and build your strength
to hold on in the whirl.

Morning's a reminder of renewal.
Things turn and change in the dark.
As we shed skin and renew cells
in our sleep,
life refreshes our circumstances,
and our ability to adapt.

To life, which is a circle.
Held by grace, which is at the middle.
And at the beginning, and the end.
The central point of the turntable,
and all of its circumference,
and everywhere we stand.

' Trust in the Lord forever,
for the Lord, the Lord himself, is the rock eternal.'

Isaiah 26:4 (NIV)

LENT SPEAK

Lent, speak to me.
A word that holds such hidden depths.

Take me on your hallowed ground,
untouched, and unturned
yet by heart or mind.

Show me your intents,
what you're yet to unveil.
I wait here still with bated breath,

to hear your name revealed.

Lent,
lead me on.
Winter I know is a season

through which we all must pilgrimage.
I am told your name means 'Spring'.
I wait for you to blossom.

Though the deserts an experience
we all must endure,
Lent teaches us to delve for life

when there's no evidence of it at all.

For Lent
in truth is life.
And just as we come to our birth

through a dark passage,
grown to fullness
hidden from the world,

so Lent teaches us
to sow in tears and then reap.
To wait in the wilderness,

until Easter springs at our feet.

'Those who sow with tears will reap with songs of joy.'

Psalm 126:5 (NIV)

SEPTEMBER

New leaves, lavender stems,
buds on the climbing rose, dew on the grass.
Lit by a sun emerging from a sky of soft blue,
as eggshell, or a new-born's gaze.

I see all this as something all of a sudden new,
unveiled to eyes that had winter's blinkers on.
How long had the yellow spring rose been bursting its buds so tight?
And when did all the trees regain their leaves?

The grass has taken on a new shade of ripest green,
while the sun's caress now bares my arms and legs,
to feel its growing warmth upon my skin.
Skin that feels as new as the season.

I shed my winter's ills and a mind that thinks in past tense,
and take hold of the promise that we are given
at the beginning of a new day,
new season, year or passageway.

Whoever said death was the last word,
has never seen God's temple against a wide sky,
or worshipped at the altar of this earth,
where his glory is reflected in fragments that we can dissect.

Yes, this spring speaks to me of life.
The earth grows ever old as it spins on its axis,
while the universe is expanding all the time;
like new leaves on my old Hydrangea's wood.

Yes God is seen in both the great and the small.
And his gift to us is always life.
Though the earth might circle the sun a million more times,
or it may not, life will not grow old, but renews itself.

'How beautiful are your tents, Jacob, your dwelling places, Israel!
Like valleys they spread out, like gardens beside a river,
like aloes planted by the Lord, like cedars beside the waters.
Water will flow from their buckets;
their seed will have abundant water.'

Numbers 24:5-7 (NIV)

THANK YOU – AN EASTER REFLECTION

Everything is thank you
if you look carefully.

The trees that lose their leaves
still raise their limbs.

The earth farewells the sun
and moves around again.

Those we love draw tears and smiles from us
in unison.

Everything is grace
and begins again.

We know this because each new day
speaks of redemption.

Because Peter denied his friend
and was forgiven.

Because the sleep that restores us,
in a small way reflects the resurrection.

Each small death brings life,
and each gift of surrender is an offering.

A down payment
for the new day coming.

For every Friday is followed
by a Sunday.

And every empty grave
formerly held something.

Yes everything is thank you
if you look carefully.

Everything in nature, love and life
reveals the resurrection.

He who bore our sin, pain and grief
lives again.

And our cross, so hard to bear,
we find lifts us to heaven.

Yes everything that happens we can thank him.
For we know our story lives in his
without an ending.

'Yours, Lord, is the greatness and the power
and the glory and the majesty and the splendour,
for everything in heaven and earth is yours.
Yours, Lord, is the kingdom;
you are exalted as head over all.'

1 Chronicles 29:11 (NIV)

THE REMAINS OF THE DAY

You have resurrected me.
You, who rose once and for all,
lean down each new day,
restore me with your loving hand,
replace me where I stand.

You, who have resurrected me,
have taught me how to rise,
to undo all the ropes,
and the remains of the day
which keep me tied.

You, my resurrection,
are my high and holy place.
From which I can see
from a different vantage
and renew my perspective.

You, who are resurrected,
teach me how to follow.
Show me where my eyes
and heart must rest,
lead me to living waters.

You, my resurrection,
restore me to your side.
And cleanse me
from the ashes
of the days left behind.

'Jesus said to her, "I am the resurrection and the life.
The one who believes in me will live, even though they die;
and whoever lives by believing in me will never die. Do you believe this?"'

John 11:25-26 (NIV)

A LADDER

I will climb to you
by a ladder,
made from the days
I've put behind me
and those I'm yet to live.

When the sun is hard
to find
I will then add a rung,
and it will lead me higher still
to seek its dawning light.

I can climb to you.
Although you're never far,
you are always that bit ahead,
guiding me forward
another step.

Yes, you have given me a ladder
and taught me to build.
My days, the material
from which I draw
perpetual wood.

When the sun is hard
to find,
or the mist hangs low
obscuring the view,
what comfort it is yet to know

I can climb to you.

'And many peoples will come and say,
"Come, let us go up to the mountain of the
Lord, to the house of the God of Jacob;
That he may teach us concerning his ways,
and that we may walk in his paths."'

Isaiah 2:3 (NIV)

BORNE UP

There are some days
in which,
just as the sun travels from east to west
across a blue horizon,
I find myself
held up,
carried aloft,
that my clay feet might not touch
the ground.

I did not know I was so light,
or inclined to be absent.
Rather I think it is that you instead
are strong and ever present.
And that it is your pleasure
to uphold us,
to assure us of the comfort and strength
found in the centre
of your arms.

And so I rest,
like a child weaned.
I have found, standing still
what many might travel the earth
on weary feet to seek,
not knowing that strength is found
where weakness gives us away,
always at our knees.

'Blessed be the Lord, who daily bears our burden,
the God who is our salvation. '

Psalm 68:19 (NIV)

COLOUR

You paint
such colour on my skin
that where I saw white
in my mirror's reflection,

I look again,
and you've unearthed them,
the colours of my soul.

I see indigo
and yellow,
but not the sallow
shade of skin,

but bright
like a finches breast
or sunflower's glow.

And there's blue and rose,
pink across the cheeks,
in such hues that
I can longer see me - for you.

Is that what you were wanting?
Is that what you would seek
to unveil?

Sometimes we
must surrender
strength in mind and body,
and decrease.

While we might appear,
by all intents and purposes
to recede,

the colours of our soul
are only reaching

the light of day.

'Lord, I am not high-minded : I have no proud looks. I do not exercise
myself in great matters: which are too high for me. But I refrain my soul,
and keep it low, like as a child that is weaned from his mother: yea, my
soul is even as a weaned child.'

Psalm 131 (NIV)

YOUR EMBRACE

Today you put your arm around me
and I heard you say,

'It is here, has been here, and here will remain.

When you close your eyes
and become still,
you hear the birdsong you did not hear before.

When you lie afloat on the ocean's depths,
you cannot stay buoyant
without allowing your body to rest.

So it is with my embrace,
still yourself in quietness
and you will feel its weight.

Centre yourself in my love
and it will become
the grace that surrounds.

I am here, always without and within.
As a warming summer sun,
though winter's drawn its curtain.

As the life that surges,
though weakness and dependence
bring you to surrender.

As the light that shines in the dark,
though the dark might appear
to have increased in strength.

Its depth is needed to highlight
the lengthening shadows
illuminating the light.

Contrast is our friend.
Without which we wouldn't see
a sun cresting upon the horizon.

And no-one would be drawn to me
without a need they need met.
Without the pull of gravity arresting their heart.

Yes, today I put my arm around you
and I hear you say,

"I feel its weight,
although it has been here all along,
today I am aware of it.'"

*'For I am convinced that neither death nor life, neither angels nor demons,
neither the present nor the future, nor any powers,
neither height nor depth, nor anything else in all creation,
will be able to separate us from the love of God that is in
Christ Jesus our Lord.'*

Romans 8:38-39 (NIV)

NOT HEAVY

They are not heavy,
the seasons of change,
which pass
like the passing weather.

We can sit outside
and watch the night turn to light,
the clouds give way to emerging day
to remember this.

On a morning that
the rain fell
and the sun shone her face
in the space of one small hour.

In which
the birds woke to sing,
I am reminded that the important things
can indeed be depended upon.

For it's true
that if the birds wake
and the sun rises,
what else is there to want?

All else passing ships
that we can grasp at,
or watch process
across the blue.

No, they are not heavy,
the seasons of change.
Not like the load of those things
we are meant to hold.

Like this good book now
open upon my lap,
and the jasmine's weight
against the fence.

'Come to me, all you who are weary and burdened,
and I will give you rest.
Take my yoke upon you and learn from me,
for I am gentle and humble in heart,
and you will find rest for your souls.
For my yoke is easy and my burden is light.'

Matthew 11:28-30 (NIV)

THIS WILL PASS

This too will pass.

This will pass like the sun rising.
This will pass like a breath of wind
across the face of a leaf.

Like the butterfly
who just this morning came
in a flash of bright colour, and then went.

It will pass.

Those things you worry at now
with the tip of your tongue.
Lift up, and weigh, and heavily put down.

They will pass.

The things sore yet
and burdensome upon your heart.
They will catch the wind and graciously depart.

They will pass.

And behind, in their wake,
might come more things.
But you know this, just as you know yourself adequate.

For all things pass.

The butterfly reminds you of this,
as does the falling leaf.
And the rising sun, warm now,

upon your upturned cheek.

'So we fix our eyes not on what is seen, but on what is unseen, since what is seen is temporary, but what is unseen is eternal.'

2 Corinthians 4:18 (NIV)

TO FOLLOW

Following is not so hard.
It's following the bird's call back to its branch.
It's following the crest of the wave back to where it breaks.
It's following the sun's eventual descent
and the stars charted tracks.

It's walking forwards,
and then often back.
In circles, or figure eights.
It's taking a detour, for a visit or a view.
It's forgetting and then retracing steps.

Following is not hard.
It's following the river's fall into the crevice.
The tree line to the ridge.
The change of vegetation
to each mountain's peak.

It's listening, and it's seeing.
Tracing feelings, and following thoughts to their origins,
or to where they peter out and dissolve.
It's feeling the stones edge, the smooth pebble,
or rough face of rock.

It's holy listening, seeing, sensing.
A pilgrimage where our outward steps
reflect the labyrinth within the heart.
Where Nature's breath slows our own,
causes us to pause and match the rhythms of grace.

Following is hearing, and recognising our yearning
as a call in the bush from one bird to another.
Registering the response to our heart's pain,
and our souls cry to connect,
with one who hears our call and responds with his.

Following is finding our way,
where we thought we had become truly lost.
It's discovering there is no place he is not.
That where the light dissolves
we turn around and find it ascending.

The one we follow is always reappearing.
We follow his feet.

'When he has brought out all his own, he goes on ahead of them,
and his sheep follow him because they know his voice.'

John 10:4 (NIV)

DIVISION

Roads are made to be walked.
Seas to be parted
where they divide with the land.

Seeds to break
and burst
so their growth can commence.

Flower buds to
blossom and bloom
that their beauty may pour forth.

And we?
We are like the African Lily's bud.
We start out small,

but with a pre-conceived design
we grow
and push at the seams of our covering.

Until at a time
set by a clock only nature knows
we break open to fruition.

Roads are made to be walked,
not stood upon.
We were not made just to look forward.

But to trust
the process which is subject
to laws larger than us.

To trust in the sea,
how it meets the land
and wraps around it.

To notice the seed,
how it grows from nothing
to become the harvest in our hand.

'For he divided the sea before them, and led them through!
The water stood banked up upon both sides of them! In the daytime he led
them by a cloud, and at night by a pillar of fire. He split open the rocks
in the wilderness to give them plenty of water, as though gushing from a
spring. Streams poured from the rock, flowing like a river.'

Psalm 78:13-17 (NIV)

BEAUTY

Beauty falls like rain,
we can't catch every drop,
but we stand still with mouths open
to slack our aching thirst.

Beauty grows like leaves
on the greening tree,
we try to grasp the outline of each stunning leaf, but can't.
Our eyes can only take in so much.

Beauty rolls in like waves
on a beach awash with driftwood,
we can't contain the blue sky that frames our sight,
nor trace each shape of silver wood.

But the rain falls,
and the leaves keep turning on the trees,
and one wave follows the next,
even when we're not present to witness.

The mountains still stand
and the kereru sing in the bush,
though there are no ears to listen.
Beauty is for beauty's sake alone.

And if we happen to capture it,
we can consider ourselves thrice blessed.
By beauty, the God who gifted it,
and not least for being given the eyes to see.

We can take a breath of gratitude and relief.
It will be here
when we are once again in sight of it.
It will not have left.

'....but when completeness comes,
what is in part disappears.'

1 Corinthians 13:10 (NIV)

PRAYER

Do my prayers find you?
I do not know,
but I know I feel better for the praying.

Do my prayers reach heaven?
I cannot say,
except that I see things changing.

Do I hear you and not my own voice?
I can't confirm,
yet I know my wisdom is not yours.

Do I believe in a deity outside me
that holds my life
as precious?

Or do I believe more
in a power within
that sustains me from the inside?

I do know
that when I wake
I breathe in unison with another,

that at once hears the prayers I breathe
and those I think,
before they are even uttered.

I know because I feel known,
and that the prayers I speak to reach you,
find me.

And the prayers I lift to heaven
echo far
in the chambers of my interior.

And the prayers others offer for me
find me quickening within
to a moving,

that can only be your presence.
Lord, whose name is Wisdom,
and Prince of Wholeness,

welcome.

'For a child has been born—for us! The gift of a son—for us!
He'll take over the running of the world.
His names will be: Amazing Counselor, Strong God,
Eternal Father, Prince of Wholeness.
His ruling authority will grow,
and there'll be no limits to the wholeness he brings.'

Isaiah 9:6-7 (NIV)

119

A MILLION GRACES

In all our efforts that attempt and fail,
there is a grace for that.

In all the ways we've loved and not loved,
there is a grace for the lack.

In all the ways we've poured out our strength
and come up spent,

or have swallowed bitterness,
and carried guilt,

there is grace.

Plentiful and bounteous
to counter our inadequacies,

to make up the space between
what is and isn't.

To bridge each glaring gap.

Yes, we can take a breath
and exhale it.

For it's in the giving up
and the release of our grip,

that we encounter the grace
made to meet each need.

Where we find the spaces that echoed
are filled,

with a grace that overarches
and undergirds.

A grace in which our deficiencies
are offset,

by the knowledge of a love
which turns lack on its head.

Yes, God is love,
and there is grace for each need.

Let us come to the font
and be filled.

'For from his fullness we have all received, grace upon grace.'

John 1:16 (NIV)

AT MY HEARTH

Somehow,

although I recognise you can still
arrive swift as flood or fire,
somehow I think you come
more often through the back door.

While I seek out signs and wonders
you've already appeared,
and at the altar of my heart
have lit the hearth.

And my house,

to which you sit expectant
of my hospitality,
may not rival other structures
built to hold your glory;

so neither does
the forest's roof and floor,
yet it holds a thousand species
within its flora and fauna.

So I think perhaps

my home might be good enough for you.
The Pentecostal flame,
that manifests your Spirit's sudden coming,
is not just witnessed in a strike of lightening,

but more often perhaps
as the slow building burn,
of a fire set with kindling
upon which your breath has blown.

'Moreover I will make a covenant of peace with them;
it shall be an everlasting covenant with them:
and I will place them, and multiply them,
and will set my sanctuary in the midst of them for evermore.'

Ezekiel 37:26 (NIV)

LOVE SURROUNDS

You surround us.
There is comfort there.

So much comfort to be had
by the thought of our
encompassment.

We lie like seeds in the earth,
or wait, as birds in a nest.

For our provision.
For our establishment
in the ground.

And for a while there
we thrive.

Until seasons change
and our understanding
grows to find,

that none of us were made to stay grounded
for long.

Birds take flight.
Seeds and green leaves are shed, and spread
across land and sky.

We were made to grow,
and lengthen and expand.

To break our shells,
to green and die,
and then restore ourselves from the ground.

And in the dark and light,
in the summer, and in the winter's night;

we recognise wherever we are,
there is a greater purpose,
and meaning profound.

Truth deeper than we might ever grasp,
found in the knowledge of your love.

Love as a tent,
that circles and surrounds.
Seen in the flight of birds, and spring's first emergent growth.

And witnessed in the dying of the light,
and the closed eyes of those farewelled.

Love is bigger, and larger and completely beyond
what we can comprehend, but its comfort
is in the knowledge that it's a tent,

and we're held safe
in its confines.

'Whoever dwells in the shelter of the Most High will rest in the shadow of the Almighty. I will say of the Lord, "He is my refuge and my fortress, my God, in whom I trust." Surely he will save you from the fowler's snare and from the deadly pestilence. He will cover you with his feathers, and under his wings you will find refuge; his faithfulness will be your shield and rampart.'

Psalm 91:1-4 (NIV)

A CANOPY

I will rest under your canopy.
Branches letting in just enough light
that I am shaded
but able to feel the sun.

I will rest under your weight.
Providence allowing just enough pressure
that I might burst my seeds
and learn my strength.

I will rest under your care.
My harvest, the simple pleasures
of living at peace within your domain,
and lining its walls with praise.

'They will be God's holy people. And the land will produce for them its lushest bounty and its richest fruit. Then the Lord will provide shade on all Jerusalem – over every home and all its public grounds – a canopy of smoke and cloud throughout the day, and clouds of fire at night, covering the glorious land, protecting it from day time heat and from rains and storms.'

Isaiah 4:4-6 (NIV)

GIVE OR TAKE

Your hand grasped mine
the moment I took it,
never mind it has been half
a life time since,

give or take.

Your hand was outstretched
long before I held it back.

And I have learned
that whether we give or take from you,
or one another, your grip stays firm and constant.

On its hold I depend alone
when all else, even my own self,
wavers in its strength
as a candle by an open window pane.

Give or take,

your hand is outstretched
to hold up all who fold without support.

All who linger without a light.
As darkness falls your hand leads on,
so that give or take, loss or gain, we need not be without a way.

Yes, your hand grasped mine
the moment I took it,
never mind it has been half
a life time since,

give or take.

And day with you, I have found,
is always rising over the brow of the next hill.

All who heed the voice of love
can take your hand,
proffered out,
give or take the strength of their own,

and know your constant, lasting love.

> 'And those he predestined, he also called;
> those he called, he also justified;
> those he justified, he also glorified.'

Romans 8:30 (NIV)

RIVER OF LIFE

Whether I live or die
it's all for you.

I live and die in vain
when I seek anything
beyond what you've ordained.

The secret is to be content.

To travel as far within as without.
To swim in the current that
brought me here.

And then without doubt
I will follow it out.

'Then the angel showed me the river of the water of life,
as clear as crystal, flowing from the throne of God and of the Lamb.'

Revelation 22:1 (NIV)

TONIGHT WHEN I STEPPED OUT

Tonight when I stepped out

and beheld the moon,
full and white
and blooming
against the dark canvas of the night,

I felt a tug,

a pull to a place that I knew.
That I might call home,
although I know not from where
it comes, this sense of knowing.

But still I feel it every time

that I am pulled beyond myself
by the moon, or the sea,
or a mountain standing strong and solid
in the ground.

It's as though all that underpins life

is suddenly written
in vivid hieroglyphics across the sky,
or the sea, or the landscape's
sweeping terrain.

And prayer,

and my heart,
seems too small to take it all in.
The only way I can is to dissolve,
to become one with all that I perceive.

Perhaps that's why

I said to my love
when I stepped outside tonight.
'Farewell, it's been so good,
I am flying to the moon.

Meet you on the other side.'

'Praise him, sun and moon; praise him,
all you shining stars.'

Psalm 148:3 (NIV)

INCOMPLETE

Everything
is incomplete Lord.
We live with things in perpetual suspense.

Like curtains open a chink
to let in the light,
so we see yet just a partial glimpse.

We live with things unresolved,
each moment a different state
of growth or decay, increase or decline.

We have a hand in creating things
that will one day dissolve,
in the hands that made them.

We have dreams and longings that
are still seeds to be planted,
in a ground yet to be prepared.

We are limited in our vision and perspective
and resistant to the things
which must of necessity conclude.

And we are so impatient
for things to start, or heal or mend,
for things to reach fruition.

For prayers to be answered
in the way we understand or expect,
as though God were at our bidding,

and subject to the demands
of our wills and hearts.
But praise God he is not limited to our vision.

For where we see a chink of light
he sees the whole vista,
and where we hold a seed, he sees a tree at its full height.

Yes, if he can wait then so can we.
And we can remember in letting go,
that one season leads on to the next.

And our palms can only hold so much
at once.
The rest decomposes to become mulch and seed.

*'Now to him who is able to do immeasurably
more than all we ask or imagine,
according to his power that is at work within us...'*

Ephesians 3:20 (NIV)

INCOMPLETE II

If

we are all shadows on this earth.

If we pass away in a breath,
and dissolve like water
at the end of our life's breadth,
but for our spirits.

If

we are all shadows,

then what do we build, that has any worth?
What do we make that we can keep?
What has eternal value
in a world of impermanence?

If

we are shadows,

then there is a light
behind and beyond us,
that defines our outline.
That casts us into a form that we can recognise.

If

we are shadows

then we together
make a picture of what is to come.
We are the drawing board
for a master design still to be outworked.

If

we are shadows

then there is something of substance
that marks out our outline on the wall.
Our spirits live, while our
bodies wane with each breath we draw.

So what do we build, that has any worth?
That lasts beyond this time and place.
If we are his Church, of which the walls
will one day fall away,

then I wonder if it might be
our body and our hands,

indwelt by his Spirit
that make up the building and the roof.

And will remain when all else dissolves like shadows,
at the end of the day.

> 'For by one sacrifice he has made perfect forever
> those who are being made holy.'

Hebrews 10:13 (NIV)

TRUST

I laid down today
and you laid with me.
My eyes closed inside,
although I was resting upright.

My grasp loosened,
my hold let go.
If this is what it's like to die
or be at peace with not knowing, then good.

I trust. All is well.
All manner of things I count
to myself as worth much are,
if not well, still good enough.

And there is grace in movement
and grace still in rest.
There is life and death abundant
in each momentary breath.

There is grace in drawing in,
and in opening up.
Like a flower giving in
to the bee's appetite.

There is only life's demands now,
and the need to take a jump.
Draw the deepest breath,
and live within it.

*'This day I call the heavens and the earth as witnesses against you
that I have set before you life and death, blessings and curses.
Now choose life...'*

Deuteronomy 30:19 (NIV)

SEASONS

Seasons, if we allow them to,
will clothe us, or undo us;
or help us to shed one skin,
to take on the new.

Autumn draws me to fall down
in a heap, with the dying leaves,
but there is nothing that I need fear
on this holy ground.

Winter will draw its hood
over me,
and the stark earth
will be the crown that adorns.

Until spring comes and I unfurl
to reach towards
a warming sun,
seeds bursting to emerge.

And summer will bring me full circle again.
We need have no fear,
even now.
The leaves speak of life beyond these times.

We are to only hold our breath, and live in quiet expectation
of all the seasons bring.

"As long as the earth endures, seedtime and harvest,
cold and heat, summer and winter,
day and night will never cease."

Genesis 8:22 (NIV)

LEARNING TO DIE

Oh Lord, if I can die to you in the little things,
I can then die when it counts.

When it matters if I let go,
or hold on.

When all that matters
loses its meaning,

in the bigger gain.

Oh Lord, if I can practice letting go today,
then tomorrow I will with ease,

cross over,
feel the curtain brush against me.

Although I will have stepped from my
skin,

discarded as a set of clothes.

Nothing to hamper my rise
into the heavens.

Nothing to keep me weighted
to the ground.

If I can die to you right now
then I can die to you,

when it's time.

Oh Lord, if I can learn to live in the little things
then I can live when it counts.

When it matters how I let go,
so that I leave nothing behind.

When all that matters
will be that I have learned to live,

by dying to the finite things

to exchange them for the infinite.

'Jesus said to her, "I am the resurrection and the life.
The one who believes in me will live, even though they die."'

John 11:25 (NIV)

BIRD ON A WIRE

Bird on a wire,
were you aware you were God's word to me today?
My Sunday sermon, against a blue sky.
His word expressed in turn of beak,
and fluff of feathers.
The language of his spirit, in the song
from your breast.

Bird on a wire,
did you know,
that your clear tune across a blue canvas
wrote his word on my heart,
as if the pen were your instrument.
Yes, we have missed your crystal clarity
in our human discernment.

Before any issue from your bill
you stood in watch,
a silent sentinel,
teaching us
we are to sing to him who made us,
from where we stand still
in reverence.

'Look at the birds of the air; they do not sow or reap or store away in
barns, and yet your heavenly Father feeds them. Are you not much more
valuable than they? Can any one of you by worrying add a single hour to
your life?'

Matthew 6:26 (NIV)

PART 3: SHOUT

'Shout for joy to the Lord, all the earth,
burst into jubilant song with music;
make music to the Lord with the harp,
with the harp and the sound of singing,
with trumpets and the blast of the ram's horn—
shout for joy before the Lord, the King.
Let the sea resound, and everything in it, the world, and all who live in it.
Let the rivers clap their hands, let the mountains sing together for joy;
let them sing before the Lord...'

Psalm 98:4-9 (NIV)

COME

Come, break my heart open

as the sun shines through the cloud
and glints off snow.

Burst into my darkness.
Don't wait for me to stop,

to remove my shoes,
or bend upon my knees.

Instead take me now, as I am.
Don't be slow,

but tear my heart asunder,
and turn it inside out.

Show me how the things within
transform to your touch.

Come into my bedroom window
in a kaleidoscope of light.

Come, don't be gentle
but fill me with your awe.

Break my heart until it spills
in shards upon the floor,

of a thousand colours
that I've never even seen.

Show me that's there's more
than I've yet imagined.

Just like the sky,
split me to the core.

And as the clouds are
turned to gold in your light,

find out any rivals
that might try to out do you.

Yes, turn me inside out
and break my heart.

'Place me like a seal over your heart, like a seal on your arm;
for love is as strong as death, its jealousy unyielding as the grave.
It burns like blazing fire, like a mighty flame.'

Song of Solomon 8:6 (NIV)

AWAKE

To awake to you
is my prayer.

I don't want to miss a moment
asleep,

if I can be more aware of you
near.

To be close in proximity
but ignorant of your presence -

what grief.

Instead,

I want to be as a bird alighting on a branch,
or a leaf on the wind.

Always in tune
with the bearer of the elements,

and depending
on your provision.

Not walking without
the intention

of taking you with me.

To awaken to you
is my prayer.

A world with senses dulled
is a world bereft.

A world that cannot
see beyond its own self,

misses all the rest
that you would give,

gifts laid unclaimed at our feet.

A world that can't see
beyond the church walls,

or the self's prison,
cannot see itself lit up

against the sky;
with the angelic host of saints,

and creeds,
which together make the body

of Christ.

To not see ourselves in him,
and him in each other -

what loss.

Lord wake us up.

*'This is why it is said: "Wake up, sleeper,
rise from the dead, and Christ will shine on you."'*

Ephesians 5:14 (NIV)

CLEAN SLATE

Morning
comes to everyone.
Blank like a canvas prepped
for the day.

And the gift we are
given at each morning's fresh start
is the freedom
to decide.

I want to pick colours today
that reflect your light,
and everywhere
write your name.

'It is good to praise the Lord, and make music to your name, O Most High,
proclaiming your love in the morning and your faithfulness at night.'

Psalm 92:1-2 (NIV)

STILL GOOD

'Good'.

Has such a small full word
ever existed?
"It is good", he first proclaimed,
when the earth was laid.

It has ever been good
as the centuries have progressed,
and the play of time
run its course.

Goodness has unravelled
as a ribbon,
on the heels of a humanity
made in his image.

Though we have sought to pierce
the heart of goodness,
'Good', the small full word,
was already established.

For our 'Good News',
Christ with God, already existed
long before we each
were created.

Our 'Good News',
incarnate in his son,
is the light the darkness
has never extinguished.

The light in the unravelling ribbons
of our journeying,
from time's dawn to now,
is still present.

So that we can wake
each new dawn to pronounce,
"It is good",
along with him.

'For everything God created is good,
and nothing is to be rejected if it is received with thanksgiving.'

1 Timothy 4:4 (NIV)

MADE FOR HIM

He made me not for me
and not for you, but for himself.

He made me delicate, complex,
unique.

In that where I see imperfect, flawed
and inadequate,

he sees the beauty of his intent,
the potential of his design,

the splendid intricacy of his plan
come to life.

I was made for him and not for you,
or even myself.

For his pleasure
I have been breathed into existence.

That just for a moment of time
I might sing the song he's given.

That my voice and heart might inhabit the role
he's signalled as mine.

The answer to our inadequacies
is in remembering why.

When we know the answer there is no question,
for we know where our worth and purpose lies.

Our protests die on our lips
and we rest in the peace of his providence.

Yes, I was made for you God,
nothing else.

Establish me entirely as your own,
for therein is the place I find myself.

'Yet to all who did receive him, to those who believed in his name,
he gave the right to become children of God.'
John 1:12 (NIV)

A MOMENT

Happiness is here.

It's under the oak tree,
or the open sky
of blue, or stars
against the dark.

It's in the breeze
soft against my skin,
or strong enough
to blow all my efforts apart.

So that I simply am
here right now,
nothing brought to bear
on this time.

Nothing to take away even.
Not the stars or the sun
that were here before me,
and will be still, when I'm gone.

This moment alone
single and complete,
holds all the treasure
of life in an acorn.

In my child's smile
and my beloved's arms,
I find brief peace
to last a lifetime.

Even though in a breath
it is lived,
and in a breath
it's then gone.

For somehow
under each moment
time stretches its tent,
so I am caught aloft.

The stars tell me this,
and that gap in the dark
where the lit heavens
break through.

I fall into happiness,
which while momentary
depends on something
more lasting than ourselves.

Yes life is full
and I'm held complete.
This happiness found in the moment
I unwrap it.

'He has made everything beautiful in its time.
Also, he has put eternity into man's heart,
yet so that he cannot find out what God has done from the beginning to
the end.'

Ecclesiastes 3:11 (NIV)

PRAY WITHOUT CEASING

I fall asleep to my petitions,
and wake with praise on my lips,
and the sense
of something turned around
as I slept.

"I make all things new", he says.
Just like the sun
on a new day is the same,
but rises clothed afresh
in a thousand different shades.

Just as the sun makes its return
to us while our eyes
seek the closure of night,
so God works while we're yet unaware
to make something new in our sight.

As colours spread across a morning sky
branch in each direction
and point the way,
so he lies our options out like a feast
against the glory of the day.

'Behold, I am doing a new thing; now it springs forth,
do you not perceive it?'

Isaiah 43:18 (NIV)

FULL

Whatever fills our soul, God gives us that.
He is pouring wine into cups.
We are just to hold ours out.

He causes the sun to rise on all.
The earth is ours and all that's good.

And as my skin responds to the warmth
of a late winter's morning,
I see dew still on the bud
that's yet to open for its full.

And I remember, our souls are made of a substance
to retain that which is poured,

upon us without measure,
without limit or withholding.
That we might draw water as the plants,
to use and to store.

'Yes God, whatever fills our soul
you give us that.
Pour into my cup, open my buds to their full
to contain you and to trust,

in your goodness to all.'

'You visit the earth and cause it to overflow;
You greatly enrich it; The stream of God is full of water;
You prepare their grain, for thus You prepare the earth.'

Psalm 65:9 (NIV)

SUNDAY MORNING

Sunday morning
dawns anew
in the blue of my heart.

Too long thinking of things
that don't matter,
until Sunday comes in its blinding light.

And I wonder where I left them,
the thoughts I couldn't put down.

'...weeping may stay for the night,
but rejoicing comes in the morning.'

Psalm 30:5 (NIV)

TE WHARE TAPA WHA

Honour your body.
It is your waka, the vessel you navigate the tributaries of life.
It holds the treasure of your mind and heart.
It is the anchor for your spirit's flight.
Give it is full due.

Treat it with the dignity and care
that you would one who serves you.

Treasure your heart.
It has its own tributaries,
that surpass the body in which its held.
It's a gift that enables us to love beyond ourselves
but no love will match that we give ourselves.

We do well to know our heart
and keep it whole.

Uphold your mind.
It too expands beyond your sight.
It holds a wealth of knowledge and
wisdom, as a treasury of gold.
But we must be careful of how its gifts are used.

Our cleverness can lead to division with pride at its root.
We can undermine all we have worked to build.

Instead we are to tend the
connections that we make
as though they were the ties that bind us in our health.
For although we rise solitary from the ground,
our roots merge with one another in the earth.

And the health of all of us,
depends on the health of each one.

Prize your Spirit. Give it access to the source of life.
Feed it with the things that nourish it.
Orient it to its true north.
It has wings and would surprise you
with the view from up high.

As we travel home in the waka that is our body
we find our spirit is the guide at our helm.

Hinengaro, Wairua and Tinana.
Whanau that binds us all as one.
We make up a treasure greater than the sum of all our parts.
And we're to remember why we are given life.
Life is always a seed that divides, to become more of itself.

In our honouring of ourselves
we will find we will always revere others in kind.

'E hara taku toa
I te toa takitahi
he toa takitini.'

'My strength is not as an individual
but as a collective'

THESE THREE REMAIN

These three remain, faith, hope and love.

Let's teach our children
not of things which they must strive to obtain.

For one day they might find such things
to be built on sand.

To be made of such stuff
that dissolves in their hands,

when they cling too hard,
or too firmly depend.

Instead love,

in truth,
is not even a lesson

for us to pass on,
but a gift already given.

Unmerited, and without condition,
it's the foundation of faith.

And faith,

is the substance of things hoped for
and unseen.

But believed,

because the love by which we are loved
has proven them to be real.

Yes faith,

is the means by which we
can know ourselves assured.

And hope,

is the tenacity
by which we hold to all that's good.

And which without
we would not

risk, or seek, or trust,
or even love.

Yes these three things

we must give our children
if we give them nothing else.

And we give them these things
by first finding them ourselves.

'And now these three remain: faith, hope and love.
But the greatest of these is love.'

1 Corinthians 13:13 (NIV)

THE BUILDER

I am building a house.
One without walls to let the sunlight in.
One without rooms,
so we can reach out
and hold each other's hands.

And my house?
It may not even have a roof.
So that we might see
the whole expanse
of what's above, and around.

And for the floor?
I like the feel of earth.

Will you come and live
with me in my house?
It's not much, but it's built
out of all the things that last.
And made of love.

'For every house is built by someone,
but the builder of all things is God.'

Hebrews 3:3 (NIV)

SPACE

Space
when you're present
is all around you.

Space to lift your arms
out wide.
To twirl.

Space to fall
down on your knees.
To unfurl.

To recognise
that when you're present
the whole world stops too.

In that moment that you
catch your breath,
the space catches you.

'So if the Son sets you free, you will be free indeed.'

John 8:36 (NIV)

OUR PLACE

We have peace and plenty here.

Can you hear it
in the silence,
and the hum of life

in this place.

That carries like a musical refrain
from one ear to the next,
from your heart to mine.

We have love in this place.

It's in the space
where your foot lifts
and mine rests.

It's the grace to live in step.

Maybe not in sequence,
but in rhythm
like a dance.

And even when words

are crossed like swords,
or doors are locked
and feelings raw,

we have acceptance.

And so much desire
for each other's good,
that our house resembles

the strong trunk of an oak.

Whose coverage keeps us safe,
while through its branches
streams the light

of stars and sun.

That we might have freedom,
yet still navigate our way back
by day or night,

wherever we have been.

To the place of love
and grace,
where we belong.

'They will be like a tree planted by the water
that sends out its roots by the stream.
It does not fear when heat comes; its leaves are always green.
It has no worries in a year of drought and never fails to bear fruit.'

Jeremiah 17:8 (NIV)

A MARRIAGE SONG

Love
becomes such,
that in time
we can no longer define
where one of us begins and one ends.

Our lives,
as our limbs in sleep,
become like two trees
whose roots interlap,
and whose branches lengthen to touch.

We give shelter
to the young
growing beneath us,
and together we raise our limbs
towards the light.

Love
becomes such,
that each shudder upon our frame
is registered by the other.
We together are a fortress against the elements.

We've built a bower
within which we live and dance,
laugh and love,
and lay down together
upon the green grass.

'This is now bone of my bone, and flesh of my flesh...'

Genesis 2:23 (NIV)

HIS HOUSE

His house

took me by surprise,
how roomy it was.

And the view, it took in all the surrounds
and beyond what I could see.

And the doors to this house
were all open.

In fact they were hard
even to perceive.

It appeared there were no
partitions,

only pillars
and cornerstone.

And it came to me,
that the foundation was Christ.

And that we were
his Holy priests.

And the house which faced
to the east,

and to north and west,
and south,

was open to everyone
who might come.

There were no exceptions.
We all belonged

to him.

'When Jacob awoke from his sleep, he thought, "Surely the Lord is in this place, and I was not aware of it." He was afraid and said, "How awesome is this place! This is none other than the house of God; this is the gate of heaven."'

Genesis 28:16-17 (NIV)

IF YOU COULD SEE

If you could see the circle of our house,
you who have lost,
you might see that just because
they are for a moment
out of sight,
they have not gone.

No, our house is higher
and wider
in circumference,
than what we can measure
with our mortal senses,
and human minds.

If we could see the circle of his house,
we who have lost,
we might walk a little easier
knowing that he is with us.
And those we can no longer see -
just up front.

Our house is a circle.
We are all just a hands breadth away.
Our fingers, they cannot reach,
or voices cross the miles,
but we are somehow
still contained,

by the hands in which we're held.

"My prayer is not for them alone. I pray also for those who will believe in me through their message, that all of them may be one, Father, just as you are in me and I am in you. May they also be in us so that the world may believe that you have sent me."

John 17:20-21 (NIV)

WE ARE TOGETHER

We are together.
All of us here together.
No-one not our brother, or our sister.

We are together.
So much more with one another,
that in truth we make a multitude.

We are together.
Not alone, but wired for each other.
Connected by threads that cannot be unwound.

Not by those who fail to realise
the kinship at our core.
The shared humanity in which we're bound.

We are together.
Faith, and hope and love,
the enduring ties by which we're tethered.

The things that will outlast our struggles,
and remain.
The things at the heart of our defence, and our endeavours.

No, we are not alone.
No matter the distance, or the fences.
No one not our brother, or our sister.

We all belong.

"And over all these virtues put on love,
which binds them all together in perfect unity."

Colossians 3:13-14 (NIV)

ANGELS

We are angels
to each other.

My needs met in you,
and yours in me.

At the very least,
we keep each other afloat.

At peace,
and on an even keel.

Company in
each other's solitude.

Fellow travellers
on this pilgrim's road.

At best though,
I suspect God might mean

us to reflect
each other's light,

magnifying glasses
of the kind that highlight the good,

that we might shed the shame
carried as a weight

on our shoulders
for far too long.

And rise still
to greater and greater heights.

We are angels
to each other.

My uplift is your gain.
The wind beneath my wings,

the impetus
for your forward momentum.

And the view of you
against the backdrop of heaven,

is the inspiration for my own
becoming,

and my journeying onwards
into the wide and beckoning sky.

'Two are better than one, because they have a good return for their labour:
If either of them falls down, one can help the other up. But pity anyone
who falls and has no one to help them up.
Also, if two lie down together, they will keep warm.
But how can one keep warm alone?'

Ecclesiastes 4:9 (NIV)

FOREVER

Forever seems so far
and yet it is only ever ahead.
Its bridge, the days that turn,
one on to the next.

Eternity is round,
we don't travel for it to be found.
We live within its midst,
held ahead, and behind

When I wish for you eternity,
I ask for what you have.
I pray that you would know your place
as more than a point in time.

Forever is not a length of string.
It's broader and deeper than we imagine.
When we find the source of life,
we turn with it where we're standing.

"I am the Alpha and the Omega,
the First and the Last, the Beginning and the End."
Revelation 22:13 (NIV)

WHAT CAN WE BUILD?

I wonder

what are we building,
with the tools we have been given.

What can we build,
that will stand in wind and storms.

That won't perish, like the earth,
and fade like worn out clothes.

What are we building,
that will last longer than silver and gold.

That will be blessed from the ground.
That will hold its form, and outlive our days.

What are we building,
with our tools, and hands made of clay.

We, whose lives are briefer than the earth's,
what foundations can we lay

that might remain.

I wonder

if the tools we are given,
though we are so weak and human,

might in fact be stronger and more lasting
than we think.

And able to wield things of worth
much greater than we measure our attempts.

For we together make a house. And we have hearts
that, for as long as they beat, will love.

I think if willing is a prayer,
then longing, and desiring each other's good, might almost be enough.

Especially, if our clay hands and feet, then
do the work of our earnest hearts.

Yes, we whose lives are briefer than the earth's,
what foundations can we lay,

that won't in the end be measured
by their love.

'Put your outdoor work in order and get your fields ready;
after that, build your house.'

Proverbs 24:27 (NIV)

JESUS COME

It is Christmas Eve.
The eve of your birth.
Our hearts now turn to you
to re-orient ourselves
to what is true.

To what is truer
than the rush and the fuss,
of all our preparations.
Truer still, than tired
hands and hearts.

Jesus Come.

And as we count the gifts waiting under our trees,
we ask ourselves,
what can we bring you?
What do we offer
that you have not already received?

You, whose gold, frankincense, and myrrh
the magi laid at your feet.
What can we bring
that means anything to you?
To whom the angels,

sang their praise.

It is Christmas Eve.
The eve of your birth.
Our hearts now turn towards you,
and as Mary and Joseph did,
we rest on you our gaze.

We kneel like the shepherd boy
lost for words.
And our hearts and all they contain
open, and melt and run out
upon the sand.

All we are left with are
open hearts and empty hands.

Jesus, come.

'A shoot will come up from the stump of Jesse;
from his roots a Branch will bear fruit.
The Spirit of the Lord will rest on him—
the Spirit of wisdom and of understanding,
the Spirit of counsel and of might,
the Spirit of the knowledge and fear of the Lord.'

Isaiah 11:1-2 (NIV)

THE COMMUNION OF THE SAINTS

He who sits outside time
wraps us in light.

We, a globe suspended in the sky,
are circled by the saints.

We circle the centre
of our solar system's place,

in an ancient universe
growing every day.

Yet we are still firmly
and tenderly held.

Secured by laws of gravity,
and grace.

We, who sit inside time
live tied yet to the ground.

He, outside us where all is clear,
reigns in community.

We cannot know,
but sometimes have the strangest view

of a world beyond our grasp.
We sense a smile, we feel the robes

of ones gone long before.
It does not matter if we are yet to know,

enough we feel their presence.
The love of those who hold us close

in the communion of heaven.

'For we were all baptized by one Spirit so as to form one body—
whether Jews or Gentiles, slave or free—
and we were all given the one Spirit to drink.'

1 Corinthians 12:13 (NIV)

WHAT IF

What do we find when we reach the end?
That there's more beyond again.

So what might we find when we look within?
Vast starry constellations.

Clusters of galaxies to rival the mansions of the sky.
The wonder of the whole beyond us mirrored on the inside.

What do we feel when we scan the horizon?
Awed and small in comparison.

So what might we feel if we considered ourselves
not witnesses at all,

but made of the same dust, atoms and molecules
in which the stars are born?

What if the pattern of the universe
and the great map maker's charts,

encompassed even us, within the glorious
extents of his realm?

What if life were a labyrinth?
A vast circling spiral.

That when we journey to the middle
we then find ourselves back on the outside.

Yes, just as the magnitude of creation
is not limited to our vision,

perhaps the magnitude of who we are
lies yet beyond our comprehension?

While stars live and burn with no-one to name
and observe them,

we all have centres at our hearts
beyond our explorations.

Yes, larger within than without,
the next time we stop to wonder,

may we wonder at ourselves
and the continents that lie undiscovered.

Might we stop too and wonder
at a creator just as mysterious

as the universe within and without us
at which we bow in reverence.

'For in him we live and move and have our being.'
As some of your own poets have said, 'We are his offspring.'

Acts 17:28 (NIV)

WITNESS

Somewhere between the water and the sky,
the earth and the vast realms of stars,
we live.

Everything here
seems to have its purpose.
Seems to carve out its niche.

Right down to the vine
cascading in the garden.
Not a random white bloom out of place.

Here for the bees, and the butterflies.
Our pleasure in its existence,
a happy mistake.

A non-essential requirement
to its being,
and yet we're still graced.

We, who lie in the middle
between the reflected sea and the stars,
wondering of what we are a part,

part star dust, part water
and part the fertile soil
in which we are cradled,

landlocked
by our heart and lungs,
we feel the wind and want to dance.

The body that makes us human
keeps us separate from all we're not,
and yet know we're still a part.

Somewhere between the water and the sky
reflections dance,
and in the sun's rays catch the light.

It's enough to breathe and witness
each transcendent
glimpse of heaven.

Perhaps in the end that's the purpose of
existence.
We're to climb up like the vine,

and behold it.

'The whole earth is filled with awe at your wonders;
where morning dawns, where evening fades,
you call forth songs of joy.

Psalm 65:8 (NIV)

LIFE

Everything's a search for beauty,
for meaning.

Rounding the garden.
Marking the days and the turning seasons.

Drawing circles, making patterns,
ensuring continuity.

Joining gaps, filling in spaces,
that stretch out bare as empty canvases.

Each moment defined
where it eclipses the next.

Days drawn in sketches,
taking on substance in experience.

Hindsight making equations, and
drawing conclusions in significance.

From this we make a life
and determine the value of it.

The circles we draw, the patterns we make,
all depending on our own artistry.

What if beauty had no meaning,
but its own existence?

And each moment was taken and celebrated
as a singular event that won't repeat?

Would we see the pattern take shape
without our forcing it?

Like a flower opening, or the dawn rising,
we might remember that some things happen without our efforts.

Beauty
for beauty's sake.

Moments that carry their own hues,
rather than those we've attributed.

Spaces that stretch out in empty brilliance
until the light catches.

And we see all the colours merging
one into the other.

Yes, beautiful moments
that make a life.

Perfectly adequate in themselves
but which surprise in their continuity.

Both a gift, and a given,
this blessed life that we live in.

*'What good will it be for someone to gain the whole world,
yet forfeit their soul? Or what can anyone give in exchange for their soul?'*
Matthew 16:26 (NIV)

JEWELS

When we record our days
we make them real to us.

We give them shape and form
that we might learn from them.

Hindsight is God's beautifier
when we shine the lens we look through.

When we record our thanks
in pen, or thought, or praise

we establish what is good
upon the pathways of our lives.

We inlay them with jewels
of many colours.

We cement the things that further us
and cast aside what doesn't.

When we travel back
we trace God's faithfulness.

In such a way
that as we cast our line into the open waters,

we use yesterday's harvest
to gain tomorrow's goodness.

Yes, when we record our days
we make them real to us.

We sift for all the wheat amongst the chaff,
mine for all the gold to further invest it.

Gratitude brings it reward,
if only to shine a light on what we couldn't see before.

We think on what is good
and see it magnified.

We trust tomorrow
because of what we've made today,

out of all the good we polish
and then display.

'Finally, brothers and sisters, whatever is true,
whatever is noble, whatever is right,
whatever is pure, whatever is lovely, whatever is admirable
—if anything is excellent or praiseworthy—think about such things.'

Philippians 4:8 (NIV)

TREES

Look at the trees.
No matter the season
there is a lesson
held in each strip of bark,
each clinging transient leaf,
each bare branching limb.

We drink from their wisdom.

From the trees,
who ask nothing of us
but give us deep companionship.
Whose silent stance
comforts us
in a wordless tenderness.

Whose dignity raises ours.

Who has not carried grief
to the forest
and been able to lay it down.
Under the trees
who stretch out their limbs
to receive.

Transfuse us with life in a silent exchange.

Trees know,
there is no need
for explanations.
Life and death have played out
under their arching canopies.
We are known and understood.

Pretence can drop like the leaves.

Hope finds its renewal
in the greening of spring.
Joy takes root
in the abundant summer bloom.
Fall brings solace in leaves that fall
with a promise of return.

Winter's starkness recalls to us
the strength standing unencumbered brings.

Yes we look up at the trees,
and no matter the season we draw
the lesson needed.
Perhaps greater than anything
the trees teach,
is what they give

without preaching.

Space to breathe,
to rest and rise up again,
to learn the secrets of the earth.
To turn with the turning seasons,
not hold on to what's made to fall,
but wait for it to return

in a new form,
in a promised spring.

'For there is hope for a tree, if it be cut down, that it will sprout again,
and that its shoots will not cease.'

Job 14:7 (NIV)

THE OTHER SIDE

The sun shines on both sides of our world.
When it sets for you
it rises for me.

When the snow settles
in silence upon the trees
and all growth halts,

here it has blossomed
and life is rife
among bird and bush.

Yes, at the toss of a hand
the coin flips
between death's door and life's threshold.

The seasons change,
or the day's light declines
before we know ourselves.

The glow of twilight,
a last burning
before the descent of night.

A coin lies in his hand,
yet however it falls
it's right side up.

Somewhere the sun is shining still.
Held in summer's embrace
we can attest to that.

In winter's chill
and dimming light,
we need someone to recall to us,

what's on the other side.

'For to me, to live is Christ and to die is gain.'

Philippians 1:21 (NIV)

HOLY

'Where you stand is holy.

Not just burning bushes
speak of me,
but the eyes that see
the holy
in the sparrow
on the tree.

You are the holy
thing I made you to be,
as you recognise,
all you perceive
brings you back
to me.

Expansive as I am,
I also contain you
in my hand,
longing to meet you
in this still
place,

right now,
where the sparrow
dances
on the flimsy branch,
and the sun glints
on new leaves.'

'Who is like the Lord our God, the One who sits enthroned on high,
who stoops down to look on the heavens and the earth?'

Psalm 113:5-6 (NIV)

A THRESHOLD

To bless the year we live in
is to receive its blessings.

Nothing can be contained
but everything can run through us
with a river's constancy.

Rapids of fresh graces
to renew
our inner springs.

Winds of mercies
blowing out the cobwebs
and airing out our rooms.

The mind's dusty corners
and the hearts
defended places,

swept with air
as clear as the new year's
dawn.

To bless the year we open
is to unwrap its fortune.

A thousand different colours,
shapes and forms
yet to encounter.

Not resenting or deflecting,
but asking ourselves,
'What is this I'm holding?'

Treasures found in unforeseen places,
stones that might
be worth more than they look.

Griefs that carve out beauty
hitherto not imagined,
spaces to then fill with more of our joy.

Part of the joy
is anticipating
what is coming.

Standing by the threshold
and then opening.

'Because of the Lord's great love we are not consumed,
for his compassions never fail. They are new every morning;
great is your faithfulness.'

Lamentations 3:22-23 (NIV)

REVOLUTION

The night wraps about me
in a blanket of stars.
A night two thousand years hence
that your presence
graced our planet.

And yet,
the night wraps around me
with the hush of newness,
that even the angels I think must
hold their breath.

The moon,
everything here,
has that sense of things ending
and renewing.
Such that,

I'm reminded,
where you live
outside time,
everything revolves
around your name.

Just as we in our journeying
circle a sun,
the light of which sustains our life,
so in a deeper sense
you stand more central than any planet,

and are the pivotal point
at which we all start and end.

'...then I saw all that God has done.
No one can comprehend what goes on under the sun.
Despite all their efforts to search it out, no one can discover its meaning.
Even if the wise claim they know, they cannot really comprehend it.'

Ecclesiastes 8:17 (NIV)

CIRCLING LIFE

The life you have lived
and embraced
in the end holds you.

The years that have passed
do not dissolve
but rise like sap inside.

The tree planted by the river
does not thirst
or suffer lack.

The life we live holds us.
What we've given
is given back.

The love we've expressed
becomes the love
in which we're embraced.

The paths we walk
revisit again
to circle us.

The ways we have blessed
become the means
in which our blessings return.

The life we have lived
hasn't holes in it,
but fills up and overflows.

'The Lord is my shepherd, I lack nothing.
He makes me lie down in green pastures,
he leads me beside quiet waters,
he refreshes my soul.
He guides me along the right paths
for his name's sake.
Even though I walk through the darkest valley,
I will fear no evil, for you are with me;
your rod and your staff, they comfort me.
You prepare a table before me
in the presence of my enemies.
You anoint my head with oil;
my cup overflows.
Surely your goodness and love will follow me
all the days of my life,
and I will dwell in the house of the Lord forever.'

Psalm 23 (NIV)

PHOTO APPENDIX

Cover Photo: Long Bay Beach, Auckland, New Zealand (Ana Lisa de Jong)

Introduction: Hahei, Coromandel Peninsula, New Zealand (Ana Lisa de Jong)

Part 1: Still: Whenuapai, New Zealand (Ana Lisa de Jong)

Heart Song: Gisborne, New Zealand (Ana Lisa de Jong)

Tears: Taupo, New Zealand (Ana Lisa de Jong)

Be Still: Muriwai, Auckland, New Zealand (Carol Haines)

Abide: Flowering Cherry, Carol's garden, Waimauku, Auckland (Carol Haines)

Wordless: Southern Star Abbey, Kopua, Takapau, Hawkes Bay, New Zealand (Ana Lisa de Jong)

Ah: Nelson, New Zealand (Carol Haines)

Winners and Losers: Hauraki Gulf, Auckland, New Zealand (Ana Lisa de Jong)

Ascension: Peony, Ashburton, New Zealand (Carol Haines)

Falling: East Cape coastline, New Zealand (Ana Lisa de Jong)

Perfect: Waioeka Gorge, SH2, Bay of Plenty, New Zealand (Ana Lisa de Jong)

The Door: Christ Church Raukokore, Opotiki, East Cape, New Zealand (Ana Lisa de Jong)

Turn Points: New Chums Beach, Whangapoua, Coromandel, New Zealand (Ana Lisa de Jong)

Flight: Muriwai Beach, Auckland, New Zealand (Carol Haines)

We Never Know: Te Araroa, East Cape, New Zealand (Ana Lisa de Jong)

To Wait: Muriwai Beach, Auckland, New Zealand (Carol Haines)

Eden: Hahei, Coromandel Peninsula, New Zealand (Ana Lisa de Jong)

God of Small Things: Southern Star Abbey, Kopua, Takapau, Hawkes Bay, New Zealand (Ana Lisa de Jong)

Part 2: Sing: Waihi Beach, New Zealand (Natasha de Jong)

We Sing: Leigh, Matakana, North Auckland, New Zealand (Ana Lisa de Jong)

Grace: Omokoroa, Bay of Plenty, New Zealand (Carol Haines)

Heaven: Tolagoa Bay, East Cape, New Zealand (Ana Lisa de Jong)

Life is a Circle: Leigh, Matakana, North Auckland (Ana Lisa de Jong)

September: Crabapple Blossom, Carol's garden, Waimauku, Auckland (Carol Haines)

The Remains of the Day: Gisborne Botanical Gardens, Gisborne, New Zealand (Ana Lisa de Jong)

Borne Up: Muriwai, Auckland, New Zealand (Carol Haines)

Your Embrace: Hahei, Coromandel Peninsula, New Zealand (Ana Lisa de Jong)

This will Pass: Dahlia, Carol's garden, Waimauku, Auckland (Carol Haines)

Division: Long Bay Beach, Auckland, New Zealand (Ana Lisa de Jong)

Prayer: Tolagoa Bay, East Cape, New Zealand (Ana Lisa de Jong)

At my Hearth: Moutere, New Zealand (Carol Haines)

A Canopy: Muriwai, Auckland, New Zealand (Carol Haines)

River of Life: Hahei, Coromandel Peninsula, New Zealand (Ana Lisa de Jong)

Incomplete: Nelson Cycle Trail, New Zealand (Carol Haines)

Trust: Maukatia, Muriwai, Auckland, New Zealand (Carol Haines)

Learning to Die: Christ Church Raukokore, Opotiki, East Cape, New Zealand (Ana Lisa de Jong)

Part 3: Shout: Maukatia, Muriwai, Auckland, New Zealand (Carol Haines)

Come: Maukatia, Muriwai, Auckland, New Zealand (Carol Haines)

Clean Slate: Anemone, Carol's garden, Waimauku, Auckland (Carol Haines)

Made for Him: Hauraki Gulf, Auckland, New Zealand (Ana Lisa de Jong)

Pray without Ceasing: Muriwai, Auckland, New Zealand (Carol Haines)

Sunday Morning: Tawharanui Regional Park, North Auckland, New Zealand (Carol Haines)

These Three Remain: Christ Church Raukokore, Opotiki, East Cape, New Zealand (Ana Lisa de Jong)

Space: Takapuna Beach, Auckland, New Zealand (Ana Lisa de Jong)

A Marriage Song: Blenheim, Marlborough Sounds, New Zealand (Ana Lisa de Jong)

If You Could See: Muriwai, Auckland, New Zealand (Carol Haines)

Angels: Christ Church Raukokore, Opotikia, East Cape, New Zealand (Ana Lisa de Jong)

What can we Build: St Mark's Chapel, RNZAF Base Ohakea, Bulls, New Zealand (Ana Lisa de Jong)

The Communion of the Saints: Muriwai, Auckland, New Zealand (Carol Haines)

Witness: Hauraki Gulf, Auckland, New Zealand (Ana Lisa de Jong)

Jewels: Muriwai, Auckland, New Zealand (Carol Haines)

The Other Side: Muriwai, Auckland, New Zealand (Carol Haines)

A Threshold: Hauraki Gulf, Auckland, New Zealand (Ana Lisa de Jong)

Circling Life: Nelson, New Zealand (Carol Haines)

About the Author

Ana Lisa de Jong is an Auckland poet and inspirational writer, and administrator for the NZDF Chaplaincy team. Inspired by her love of God, the written word, art, nature, and people, she writes daily, for her own benefit and other's encouragement. Drawn back to writing in her 40's Ana Lisa found herself bursting forth on a 'river of words', leading to many 100's of poems, and the publication of three volumes of poetry between 2014 and 2016. Published by Lang Book Publishing, her *Poetry for the Soul* series, comprised of 'Songs in the Night', 'Hope Springs' and 'Seeking the Light', has touched and encouraged many, her grace filled writing finding the spiritual in everyday life, and revealing the loving heart of God towards each of us.

Ana Lisa, still drawing from an ever deepening and evolving creativity and prolific outpouring of words, brings this further offering to the table. 'Heart Psalms', the first volume of her new 'Poetry of the Heart' series will be followed by 'Thrice Blessed'. These large volumes of Ana Lisa' s recent writing will continue to speak, as her last volumes have done, to hearts in need of spiritual nourishment, and moments of solace and relief in an ever changing and challenging world.

Ana Lisa's words are words for today, and have had a profound impact on her many readers. Regularly writing reflections and poetry on her website and *Facebook* page, she also contributes to *Godspace* and other on-line websites, along with publications such as the *Refresh Journal of Contemplative Spirituality*. You can visit Ana Lisa at www.livingtreepoetry.com.